For my traveling companions, Eddy, Will, Clair and Lach

This book took a decade to reach publication.
Thanks to Rita Hart for sticking with it all the way.

First American edition 2005
by Kane/Miller Book Publishers, Inc.
La Jolla, California

First published by Penguin Books Australia, 2004
Copyright © Alison Lester, 2004

All rights reserved. For information contact:
Kane/Miller Book Publishers, Inc.
P.O. Box 8515
La Jolla, CA 92038
www.kanemiller.com

Library of Congress Control Number: 2004109117

Printed and bound in China by Regent Publishing Services, Ltd.

3 4 5 6 7 8 9 10

ISBN: 978-1-929132-73-7

Are we there yet?

Alison Lester

A journey around Australia

Kane/Miller

BOOK PUBLISHERS

Starting out

The year I turned eight, Mum and Dad took us on a trip around Australia. Luke, Billy and I missed school for the whole winter term.

Nan and Poppa stayed behind to look after Buffy and Tigger and Bess.

We towed Poppa's old camper trailer, and it was our home for three months. It folded out to make a little house, with a table, a fridge, two double beds, a stove and a sink. It had everything we needed.

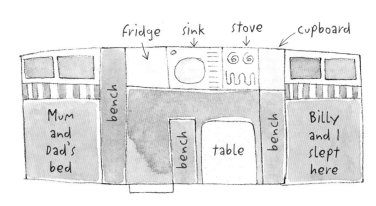

We practiced in the backyard before we left

Cross-section of our van

Luke slept in his sleeping bag under the stars except when it rained, and then he bunked in with us. We were squashed but it was cozy.

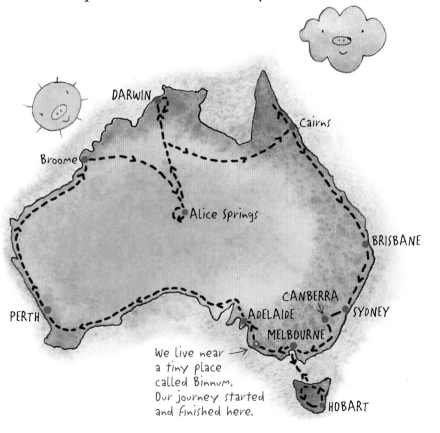

DARWIN

Cairns

Broome

Alice Springs

BRISBANE

PERTH

CANBERRA

ADELAIDE

SYDNEY

MELBOURNE

We live near a tiny place called Binnum. Our journey started and finished here.

HOBART

The day we left, I helped Nan pin up a big map of Australia so she and Poppa could follow our journey.

"I wish I was coming, Grace," Nan said, as she hugged me tight. "I'm going to miss our cuddles."

On the road at last

I waved to Nan and Poppa until Dad turned onto the road leading out to the highway. I felt sad and excited at the same time. Nobody said anything for ages, not until we reached the coast.

We saw the last autumn leaves fluttering like flags on the grapevines of the Barossa Valley.

Then, at the Coorong, Luke made us laugh. "Look," he said, "a pelican. Its beak can hold more than its belly can."

On our first night we camped on the edge of the Flinders Ranges. It felt like we were the only people in the world.

At Streaky Bay we stuck
our heads in the mouth
of a great white shark.

We made letters with our shadows
at Murphy's Haystacks. The giant
boulders glowed in the afternoon sun.

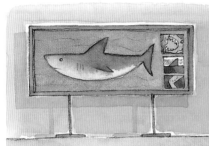

That evening at the camping
ground, Mum said Billy
had to use the women's
bathroom because he was
still little. He was embarrassed.
"Okay," he said, "but if anyone
comes in, call me Kylie."

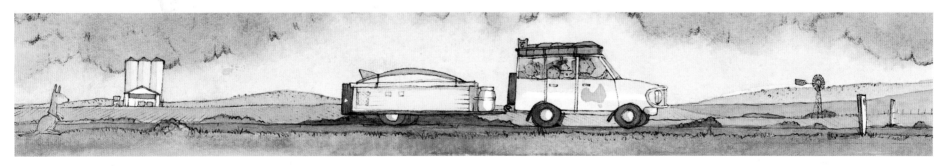

We drove past wheat silos and windmills, and Billy asked, "Are we there yet?"

It took us two days to cross the Nullarbor Plain. I waved to the people in passing cars and trucks, and they always waved back.

We all had our favorite positions in the car.

Dad loved → driving

← Luke rode shotgun

Billyville

Border

Graceland

↗ Billy and I shared the middle

Mum liked the back where she ↓ could lie down and read

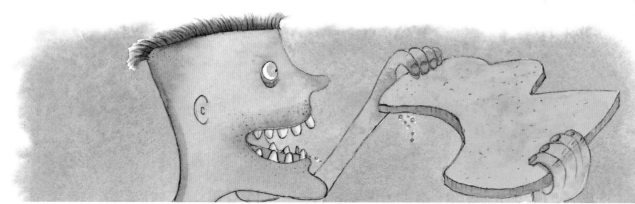

The Great Australian Bight looked like a giant had bitten a huge chunk out of Australia.
Dad and Luke stood right on the edge of the cliff, but Mum stayed back. She held on to Billy and me so tight that my hand went numb. "Ooh," she said. "I can't look."

At Head of Bight we saw ten whales in the sea below us. A mother and her calf were rolling and wallowing together. Their mournful music sounded like an underwater orchestra.
"It's making me sleepy," I said to Mum.
"They must be singing a whale lullaby."

Over the desert and into the west

At Eucla we had sandy sandwiches near the ruins of the old telegraph station. Next day, we traveled for nearly 150 kilometers on a really straight road. Dad pretended to drive with his eyes closed, but I could tell he was peeking.

Luke surfed on stone at Wave Rock . . .

. . . but Dad waited for the real waves at Rottnest Island.

The quokkas came so close to me, I could see their tiny whiskers.

After Perth, we went to see the Pinnacles.
They poked up through the sand like
giant limestone fingers.

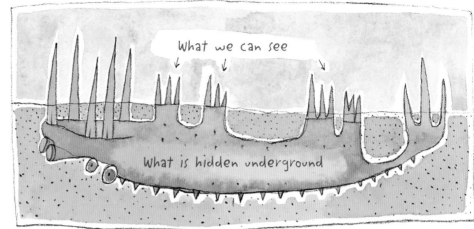

What we can see

What is hidden underground

What I think the Pinnacles really are

It was so windy at Geraldton that the trees grew sideways.

We drove past a pink tapestry of wildflowers, and Billy asked, "Are we there yet?"

The further north we traveled,
the hotter it became. We stood
in the shallows at Monkey Mia
to see the dolphins.
"Too crowded," said Dad.
"I liked it better when it was
just us and the whales."

Mum made me wear
my hat all the time.
"Hats and sunscreen,"
she'd say every time
we stopped. "This sun
will burn you to a crisp."

MY stupid hat

That afternoon, Mum and Billy and I had a picnic
in the dunes, then fell asleep like a pride of lions.
Later when we went for a dip, a dolphin came up
close and swam right between us.

We went snorkeling at Turquoise Bay.
A gentle current carried us over the coral reef,
as though the ocean was giving us a tour.
There were so many fish, like sparkling jewels.
My favorites were the tiny Blue Angels.

Turquoise Bay

The Outback

At Broome we ate crunchy fish and chips and watched the moon reflected in the mudflats of Roebuck Bay.
It's called the Staircase to the Moon.

The next day we camped at Windjana Gorge. Mum loved the boab trees. "They look like opera singers," she said. Dad and Luke called them upside down trees.

We flew over the Bungle Bungles in a helicopter without any doors, and my stomach turned inside out. "I can't look," said Mum again.

At Tunnel Creek we waded through an underground river. The dark water came right up to my armpits. When something slimy slithered past my leg, I screamed. Luke said, "Don't be such a sook."

Possible creepy things in the water

Heading south on the Tanami Track, the sand was so deep our car got stuck. Everyone felt hot and grouchy, and Mum was worried we'd be stranded in the desert. Luke found a tiny Thorny Devil, standing fierce as a dragon, and that cheered us up.

A football team helped push us out, and Billy asked, "Are we there yet?"

At Alice Springs we stayed with Mum's friend, Ruth. The days were hot, but the nights were freezing.

Ruth took us to her school and a teacher showed Mum and me how to dig for witchetty grubs. They tasted like egg yolk, runny and delicious, with a crunchy head and wriggly legs. Mum wouldn't try one. "No, thank you," she said. "I'm still full from breakfast."

Luke and Billy played footy with some of the local boys.

Noon

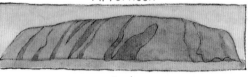
Afternoon

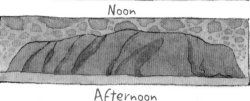
Dusk

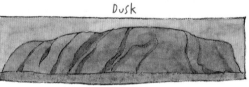
Evening

That afternoon we drove out to see Uluru.
Dad spotted it first, when we were still 35 kilometers away.
"Wow," he said. "That's a BIG rock."
At sunset we watched its color fade to purple.

We hiked between the round red domes of Kata Tjuta. The trees whispered to us as we walked through the Valley of the Winds.

Uluru is the heart of Australia.
A huge red heart, right in the middle
of the country. One day we got up early
in the cool of the morning, and walked
around the rock. I felt as tiny as an ant.

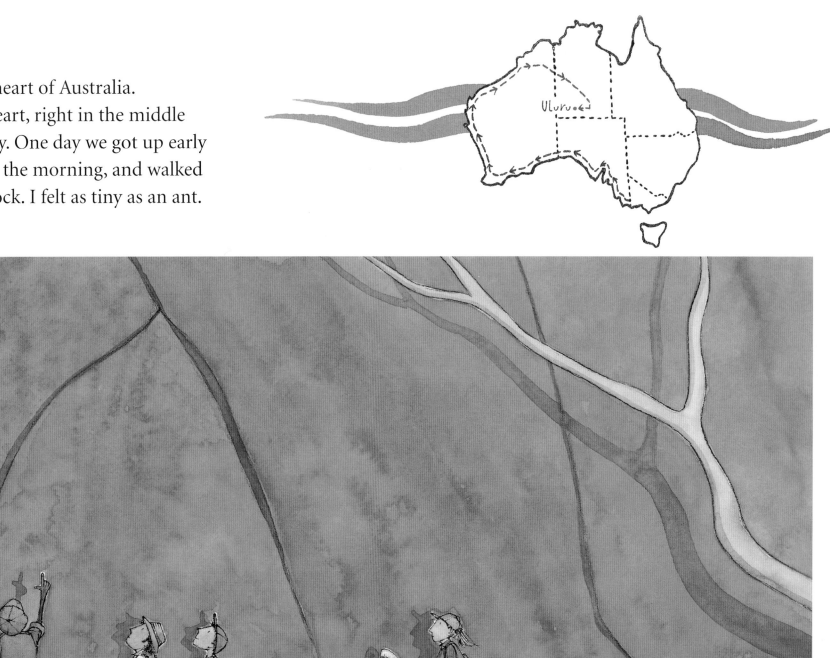

The Top End

We floated down Katherine Gorge, below towering ochre cliffs. "This is the life," said Dad. "Just wake me up if we come to a waterfall." We drifted so slowly that even a turtle swam past us.

We stayed with our cousins in Darwin, and played in their shady pool until we were as wrinkled as prunes.

At night the ceiling fans whirred constantly overhead. Even a sheet felt hot. Tiny grey geckos hunted insects on the walls.

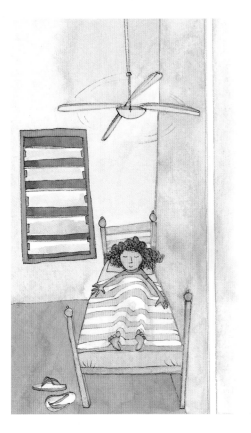

Mum and I loved the market at Mindil Beach. There was so much yummy food, it was hard to choose. We ate satay prawns and drank mango smoothies as we watched the sun set.

We drove across the floodplains, past egrets and jabiru, and Billy asked, "Are we there yet?"

At Kakadu we went on a billabong cruise. The boat drew so close to one enormous crocodile that I could count its teeth.

Luke caught a huge fish in the East Alligator River. It was so big we invited all the other campers to Luke's Barramundi Barbecue.

We swam at Gunlom where there were no saltwater crocodiles. The water was cool and silky. Dad kept diving under and grabbing my feet, and even though I knew it was him, I screamed every time.

Tony, our Kakadu guide, led us through galleries of rock art. The sandstone overhangs were alive with animals, handprints and spirits from the Dreamtime. Some of the paintings were more than twenty thousand years old. One small handprint looked just like mine.

The Far North

As we traveled on the Barkly Highway, we caught up with a big mob of cattle. We stopped to share our cool water with the dusty drovers, and the boss let me ride his horse for a little way.

Taffy was the same color as Bess and just as gentle, but twice as tall.

Near Cloncurry the Flying Doctor's plane flew over us. We invented patients for him, and Luke had the best idea: a drover who got bucked off his horse and landed on a spiny anteater.

At the circus at Mount Isa, an elephant ate my horrible hat! She swiped it off my head with her trunk and scoffed it. "Thank you, elephant," I shouted.

Dad bought me a new hat at the Mareeba rodeo. "You look like a real cowgirl, Gracie," said Mum.

This is the cracker. It makes the noise.

We met an old stockman who taught us how to crack a whip. He showed Luke how to twist the cracker.

That night, Billy and I rode our broncos until they couldn't buck any more.

The next morning, we drove through the shadowy green rainforest, and Billy asked, "Are we there yet?"

In Far North Queensland we walked beside the Daintree River. Giant butterflies landed on Mum's blue T-shirt.
"They think you're a beautiful flower, Mum," said Billy.

Luke found a snake-shaped piece of mangrove wood. He carved it into a walking stick for Poppa.
"I can't look," said Mum again.

The Great Barrier Reef was a swirling underwater carnival of fish and coral.

We went beachcombing at Cow Bay, where the jungle came right down to the sand. Mum and I made a shell mermaid together. "When the tide comes in tonight, she'll swim out to sea," said Dad. I imagined her out there, riding her dolphin like an ocean cowgirl.

Cow Bay

Heading south

In Cairns we spent all our time at the pool. One day, Mum crashed into Billy on the water slide and got banned for the whole afternoon.

At Hinchinbrook Island we hiked for hours to swim at Mulligan Falls. That evening, we were so tired and sore we all needed a back rub.

We left the coast and drove inland to visit our friends at Miles. We all helped on the farm, and Luke had a go at shearing. The sheep looked skinny and embarrassed without their wool.

At Surfers Paradise we rode
on a scary bungee ride.
"Uurgh!" moaned Dad, as it
catapulted up. "I can't look."
But Mum laughed as she
spun above the lights.
"I *can* look," she shouted.

Later that week, we caught
heaps of fish off the jetty
at Forster.

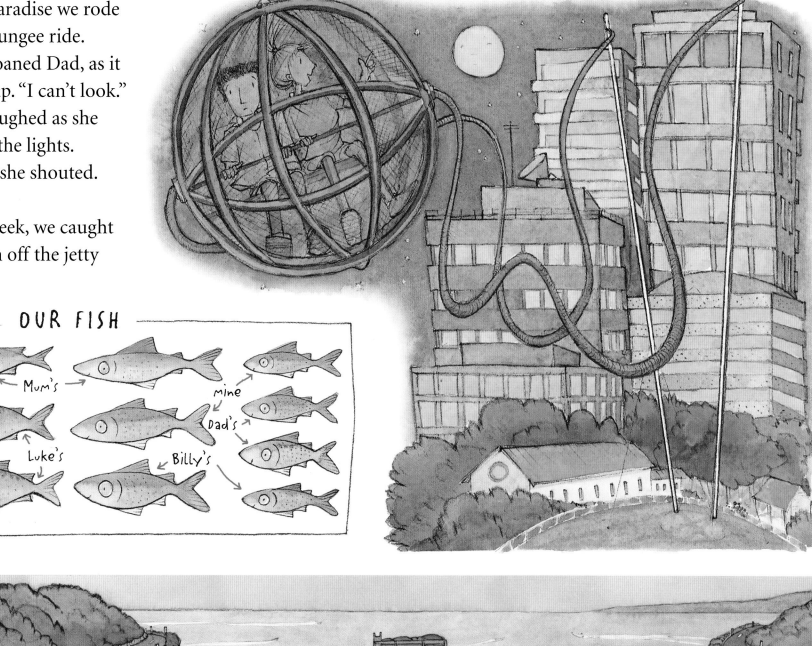

OUR FISH

Mum's

mine

Dad's

Luke's

Billy's

Boats skimmed across the sea as we drove down the coast, and Billy asked, "Are we there yet?"

When we got to Sydney we parked
our van in Uncle Pete's garden.

Next day at the zoo a baby elephant
stared hungrily at my hat so I ran.
"No way," I yelled. "I like this hat."

One day, we went bushwalking in the
Blue Mountains. Oil evaporating from
the eucalyptus trees makes the blue haze.
Mum and I imagined the kind of clothes
the Three Sisters would wear.

Uncle Pete's dog, Bongo, towed Luke
all the way along Bondi Beach.

Bongo is Buffy's brother

On our last night in Sydney we had a picnic overlooking the harbor. Cascading fireworks exploded across the sky and their reflections shimmered on the water. It felt like a farewell display, just for us.

The Cold Country

On our way to the mountains, we stopped at Canberra and spent a whole day visiting galleries. Mum and I always liked the same paintings.

Billy made a Ned Kelly helmet at Glenrowan. "Hands up!" he said, "I'm a bushranger."

Winter had arrived in the south and it was freezing at Mount Hotham. Billy and Luke and I had never seen snow before. We caught snowflakes in our mouths and wore socks on our hands to keep them warm.

We crossed Bass Strait on a big red ferry. The sea was so rough we all felt sick. Luke turned pale green.

In the Hobart museum we saw a stuffed Tasmanian Tiger. I felt sad to think they were extinct. Mum tried to cheer me up. "You never know, Gracie," she said. "There might still be a tiger family in the bush."

When we went hiking at Cradle Mountain, I kept a lookout for tiger tracks.

It rained so much we played Monopoly for hours. Luke always won, even when Dad and Billy and I ganged up on him.

At the end of the week, we drove back onto the ferry, and Billy asked, "Are we there yet?"

Wilsons Promontory is the most southerly part of the Australian mainland. I found a paper nautilus there, washed ashore at Squeaky Beach.

One evening at Phillip Island, we watched little penguins surf ashore, then waddle up the beach like tiny explorers.

Melbourne was crowded and fast after camping at the beach. The traffic noise kept me awake at night. We learned to juggle at St. Kilda.

On the last day of our trip, Dad got us up early. As we drove away from the city, I looked back at the dawn through sleepy eyes.

Winding along the Great Ocean Road, we stopped to look at the Twelve Apostles standing in the surf. The sea was wild and foaming, and we were nearly home.

The Twelve Apostles

Finally, we were back at our house.
Buffy was so pleased to see us, she jumped right into the car.
I cuddled Tigger and called out to Bess. It was good to hear her whinny back.
Billy woke up and asked, "Are we there yet?"

And we were.
We were home.